PETS TO THE RESCUE

Dolores and the Big Fire

A True Story

First Simon Spotlight edition November 2011
First Aladdin Paperbacks edition March 2003

SIMON SPOTLIGHT
An imprint of Simon & Schuster Children's Publishing Division
1230 Avenue of the Americas
New York, NY 10020

Book design by Debra Sfetsios
The text of this book was set in Times New Roman.
The illustrations were rendered in watercolor.

Printed in China
10 9 8 7 6 5

Library of Congress Cataloging-in-Publication Data:
Clements, Andrew, 1949–
Dolores and the big fire : a true story / written by Andrew Clements ;
illustrated by Ellen Beier.
p. cm. (Pets to the rescue ; #3)
Summary: A usually aloof cat risks her own life to save
her owner from a deadly fire.
ISBN 978-0-689-82916-1 (hc)
1. Abyssinian cat—Anecdotes—Juvenile literature. [1. Abyssinian cat.
2. Cats. 3. Pets.] I. Beier, Ellen, ill. II. Title. III. Series.
SF449.A28 C63 2000 636.8/26 21 99-041371
ISBN 978-1-4814-1494-4 (eBook)
1214 SCP

PETS TO THE RESCUE

Dolores and the Big Fire

A True Story

Written by Andrew Clements
Illustrated by Ellen Beier

Simon Spotlight

New York   London   Toronto   Sydney   New Delhi

Kyle lived in an old house.
For years he had lived alone.

Then he got a kitten.
He named her Dolores.

Some cats like to be
picked up and held.
Not Dolores. She did not
even like to be petted.

But Kyle didn't mind.
Kyle just liked sharing
his home with Dolores.
Dolores even ate
at the table with him.

Kyle watched Dolores
explore her new home.
He enjoyed seeing
Dolores grow.

And every time
Kyle came home,
Dolores would
meet him at the door.

Sometimes Dolores would
act like she was afraid.
Then Kyle would say,
"It's all right, Dolores.
Don't be scared."

10

At night Kyle left
all the lights on for Dolores.
It made her feel better.

One night when
Kyle was sleeping,
Dolores did something new.

Dolores jumped on Kyle's
head and scratched him.
Kyle slowly woke up.

Kyle opened his eyes
and sat up.

He thought, "I know
I left the lights on.
Why is it so dark?"

Then he knew why—smoke!
All the rooms were filled
with black smoke!

Kyle couldn't see.
It was hard to breathe.
He had to get
out of there—fast!

16

The back door was
the only way out.
Dolores stayed close to Kyle.
He started for the back door.

Kyle felt his way
along the floor.
He could feel Dolores
right next to his feet.

18

At last he made it to
the door.

When Kyle reached
for the doorknob,
it came off in his hands.
They were trapped!

Kyle pushed at the door,
but he felt weak.
He dropped onto the floor.
Kyle was all out of air.

Again, Dolores
scratched Kyle.
And again, Kyle slowly
woke up.
Kyle stood up.
He gave one last push
at the locked door.

This time, the door
gave way.

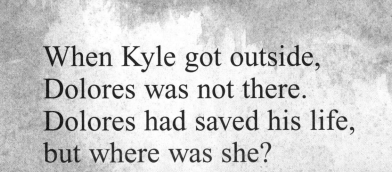

When Kyle got outside,
Dolores was not there.
Dolores had saved his life,
but where was she?

24

The firefighters
gave Kyle some air.
He felt a little better,
but Dolores was still
missing.

Three hours later
a fireman came over.
He had something
in a towel.
He said, "This was just
inside your door."

Kyle looked,
and his eyes
filled with tears.
It was Dolores.

She had been burned,
but she was still alive.
For three days Dolores
seemed almost dead.
Her eyes had been
burned shut, and a lot
of her fur was gone.

28

Then on the fourth day
Dolores opened her eyes and
drank some milk.
Kyle said, "I know Dolores
is going to make it."

Kyle took good care
of Dolores.
Slowly she got better.
Then Dolores got an award
for saving Kyle's life.

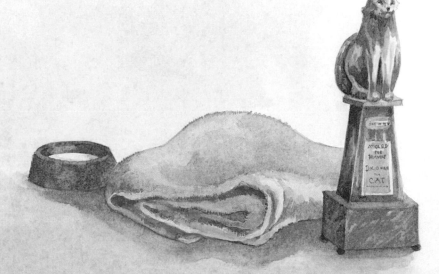

After the fire Dolores was
not so fearful.
She even liked to sit
on Kyle's lap and let him
pet her.

Kyle said, "I lost almost everything in that fire. But I didn't lose the most important things— my own life, and the life of my cat, Dolores."